BASIC TIME TELLING
INTRODUCING HOURS AND HALF HOURS PRACTICE WORKSHEETS

WORKBOOK WITH ANSWERS

A Complete Guide to Learning Basic Time Telling to the Whole Hour and Half Hour Using Various Easy to Grasp Exercises

By Shobha

VOLUME I

Table of Contents

Analog Clock Reference

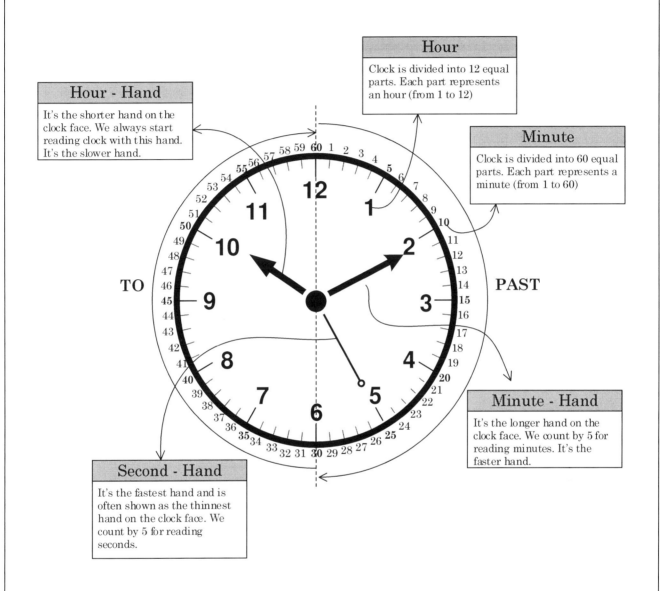

Hour - Hand
It's the shorter hand on the clock face. We always start reading clock with this hand. It's the slower hand.

Hour
Clock is divided into 12 equal parts. Each part represents an hour (from 1 to 12)

Minute
Clock is divided into 60 equal parts. Each part represents a minute (from 1 to 60)

Minute - Hand
It's the longer hand on the clock face. We count by 5 for reading minutes. It's the faster hand.

Second - Hand
It's the fastest hand and is often shown as the thinnest hand on the clock face. We count by 5 for reading seconds.

TO

PAST

In a day there are 24 hours so the hour hand has to make two complete revolutions every day.

In an hour there are 60 minutes so the minute hand has to make one complete revolution every hour. So if the hour hand traverses from 12 to 1 then the minute hand would move 60 places making one complete revolution of the clock.

In a minute there are 60 seconds so the second hand has to make one complete revolution every minute. So if the minute hand traverses from 1 to 2 (see smaller numbers on outer periphery of the clock above) then the second hand would move 60 places making one complete revolution of the clock.

Before we start practicing and acquiring this important time telling skill, we must understand that it's very simple and fun to learn time telling and it can easily be achieved with regular consistent practice. If you have a digital clock at home then even though it would be painful, try to avoid seeing time in it for some time until you are comfortable telling time with an analog clock.

Before You Start Telling The Time

Before learning to tell time it's recommended to learn the skills listed below:
- Counting up to 60
- Skip counting by 5s (5 times table) → Being able to quickly tell 5, 10, 15, 20, etc. helps understand the movement of the minute hand on a clock.
- Distinguish clock hands by their length

How To Tell Time

Closely look at the clock on the previous page. See how numbers to represent hours (big numbers) and minutes (small numbers) are laid on the clock face. Observe that each position on the clock face has two different numbers assigned to it – the big number and the small number. Big numbers are always used for telling hours and small numbers are used for telling minutes. In regular clocks smaller numbers are not marked. So how would you find minutes? Don't worry! It's very easy. You just need to count by 5s to get minutes. If you have already learnt basic multiplication, then you just multiply the big number by 5 to get the minutes. Look at the pattern below. This helps understand how minutes are progressing with each number that represents an hour.

Hour	1	2	3	4	5	6	7	8	9	10	11	12
Minute	*5*	*10*	*15*	*20*	*25*	*30*	*35*	*40*	*45*	*50*	*55*	*60*

Also remember the following

☞ **Hour Hand is shorter and mostly thicker**

☞ **Minute Hand is longer and mostly thinner**

☞ **When the minute hand is pointing at 12, it's the exact hour and no minutes have passed**

Now let's look at a step by step method to tell time

STEP – 1

Look at the clock on the right. Now find the position of the hour hand.

In this case it's between One and Two.

Take the lower of the two numbers which is **One**.
This tells us the hour of the day.

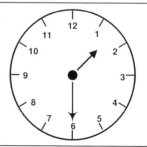

STEP – 2

Look at the clock on the right. Now find the number that the minute hand is pointing at.

In this case it's at **Six.**

This tells us the minute of the hour.

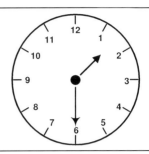

STEP – 3

Count by 5s six times. 5, 10, 15, 20, 25, **30.**

If you know multiplication, then directly get the minutes by multiplying 6 and 5. i.e. 6 x 5 = 30.

So the minute of the hour is **30**. We also call it **half-past.**

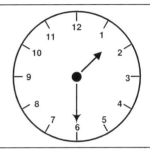

STEP – 4

Put all the information together.

→ Hour is One
→ Minute is 30 (or half-past)

So the time of the day is Half-past One.
In digital format it can be written as 1:30.

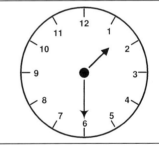

Elapsed Time

Now that we have learnt how to tell time let's take a look at elapsed time. Elapsed time is the amount of time that has passed between two events. When you hear something like "time spent", "how long", "time passed", "time difference", etc. that basically means we are talking about elapsed time. Look at the below clocks and try to find elapsed time between them.

START TIME

END TIME

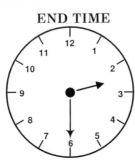

First clock shows 1:30 and the second clock shows 2:30.

START TIME = Half-past One
END TIME = Half-past Two

So the elapsed time = 1 hour.

Elapsed Time Using The Number Line

Did you know we can also represent a clock on a number line as shown below?

Now let's solve an elapsed time problem using the above number line.

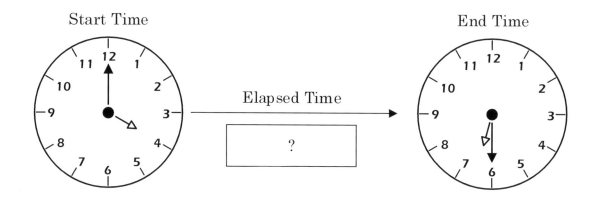

Mark the start time and end time on the number line and then see how many hops you would make from the start time mark to reach the end time mark.

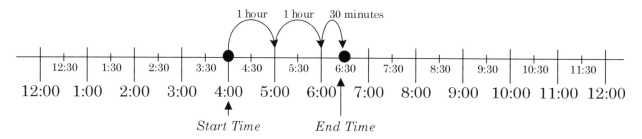

From the clocks shown above, we marked the start time at 4:00 and the end time at 6:30 on the number line.

Now let's start hopping forward starting from the 4:00 mark one step at a time.

After the first hop we are at 5:00. We are still behind the 6:30 mark. So let's make another hop to reach the 6:00 mark. Keep counting how many hops you are making as that would give us the number of hours elapsed. So after the second hop we are at 6:00 but still behind the 6:30 mark. However, this time we do not need to make another full hop as that would take us to 7:00 which is after the 6:30 mark. So make a half hop to land on 6:30.

Now let's look at the number of hops we made so far. We made two full hops from the 4:00 mark to the 5:00 mark and then from the 5:00 mark to the 6:00 mark. We also made a half hop from the 6:00 mark to the 6:30 mark. So the total elapsed time is 2 hours and 30 minutes.

Basic Time Telling – Introducing Hours and Half Hours

Date: _____ Start: _____ Finish: _____ Score: _____

What time does the clock show? Fill the box. Example: Four O'Clock.

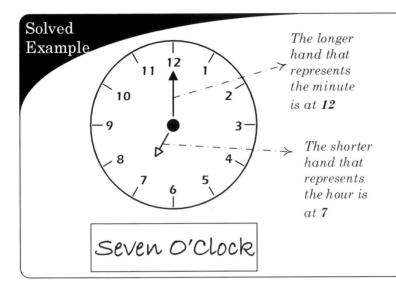

Solved Example

The longer hand that represents the minute is at 12

The shorter hand that represents the hour is at 7

Read the time shown in the clock and write down the hour in **words** in the box below.

A solved example is shown on the left side.

Seven O'Clock

1

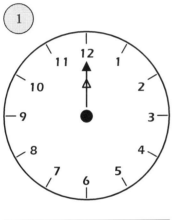

2

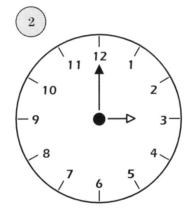

3

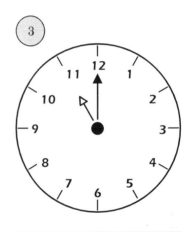

4

5

6

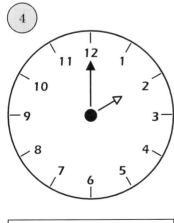

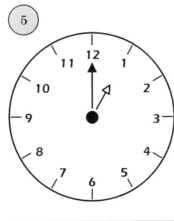

Basic Time Telling – Introducing Hours and Half Hours

Date: _____ Start: _____ Finish: _____ Score: _____

What time does the clock show? Fill the box. Example: Four O'Clock.

1

2

3

4

5

6

7

8

9

Basic Time Telling – Introducing Hours and Half Hours

Date: _____ Start: _____ Finish: _____ Score: _____

What time does the clock show? Fill the box. Example: Four O'Clock.

①

②

③

④

⑤

⑥

⑦

⑧

⑨

Date: _____ Start: _____ Finish: _____ Score: _____

What time does the clock show? Fill the box. Example: Four O'Clock.

①

②

③

④

⑤

⑥

⑦

⑧

⑨

Basic Time Telling – Introducing Hours and Half Hours

Date: _____ Start: _____ Finish: _____ Score: _____

What time does the clock show? Fill the box. Example: Four O'Clock.

(1)

(2)

(3)

(4)

(5)

(6)

(7)

(8)

(9)

Date: _____ Start: _____ Finish: _____ Score: _____

What time does the clock show? Fill the box. Example: Four O'Clock.

①

②

③

④

⑤

⑥

⑦

⑧

⑨

Date: _____ Start: _____ Finish: _____ Score: _____

Draw the hands to show the time.

Solved Example

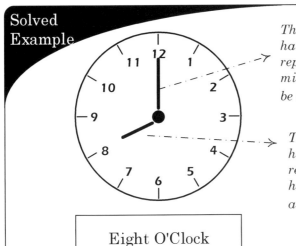

*The longer hand that represents the minute should be at **12***

*The shorter hand that represents the hour should be at **8***

Read the time shown in the box. In this case its Eight O'Clock. Now using a pencil **draw** hour and minute hands in the clock.

A solved example is shown on the left side.

Eight O'Clock

1

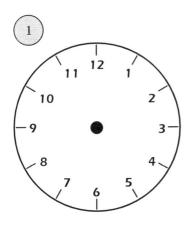

Seven O'Clock

2

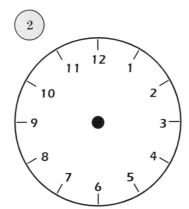

Two O'Clock

3

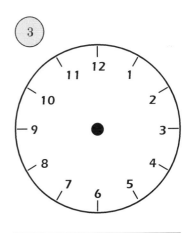

Five O'Clock

4

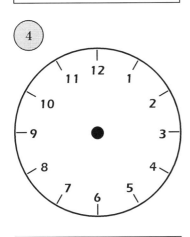

Nine O'Clock

5

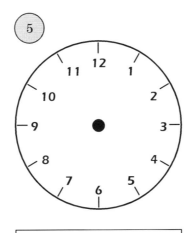

Three O'Clock

6

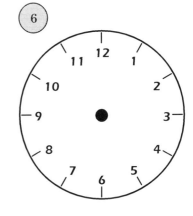

One O'Clock

Date: _____ Start: _____ Finish: _____ Score: _____

Draw the hands to show the time.

①

Four O'Clock

②

Seven O'Clock

③

Two O'Clock

④

Ten O'Clock

⑤

Five O'Clock

⑥

Three O'Clock

⑦

Twelve O'Clock

⑧

One O'Clock

⑨

Eleven O'Clock

Basic Time Telling – Introducing Hours and Half Hours

Date: _____   Start: _____   Finish: _____   Score: _____

Draw the hands to show the time.

1
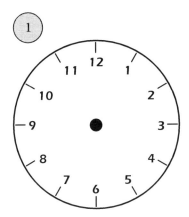

| Four O'Clock |

2

| Nine O'Clock |

3
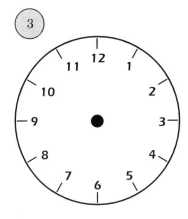

| Eleven O'Clock |

4
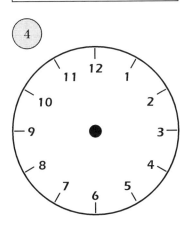

| Twelve O'Clock |

5
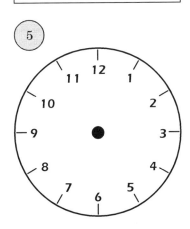

| Three O'Clock |

6
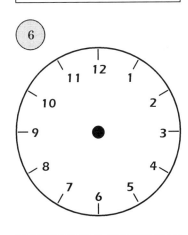

| Ten O'Clock |

7
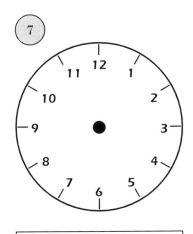

| Two O'Clock |

8
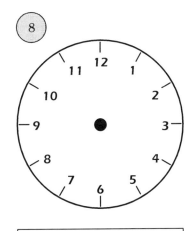

| Seven O'Clock |

9
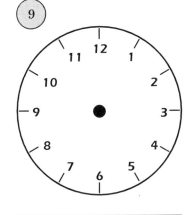

| Five O'Clock |

Date: _____ Start: _____ Finish: _____ Score: _____

Draw the hands to show the time.

①

Twelve O'Clock

②

Two O'Clock

③

One O'Clock

④

Seven O'Clock

⑤

Six O'Clock

⑥

Eleven O'Clock

⑦

Nine O'Clock

⑧

Five O'Clock

⑨

Ten O'Clock

Date: _____ Start: _____ Finish: _____ Score: _____

Draw the hands to show the time.

1

Five O'Clock

2

Eleven O'Clock

3

Seven O'Clock

4

Four O'Clock

5

Two O'Clock

6

One O'Clock

7

Three O'Clock

8

Nine O'Clock

9

Twelve O'Clock

Date: _____ Start: _____ Finish: _____ Score: _____

Draw the hands to show the time.

①

One O'Clock

②

Nine O'Clock

③

Five O'Clock

④

Two O'Clock

⑤

Three O'Clock

⑥

Twelve O'Clock

⑦

Six O'Clock

⑧

Ten O'Clock

⑨

Eight O'Clock

Date: _____ Start: _____ Finish: _____ Score: _____

What time does the clock show? Write in the box. Example: 2:00.

Solved Example

The longer hand that represents the minute is at 12

The shorter hand that represents the hour is at 5

Read the time shown in the clock and write down the hour in **digits** in the box below.

A solved example is shown on the left side.

5 : 00

1

2

3

4

5

6

Date: _____ Start: _____ Finish: _____ Score: _____

What time does the clock show? Write in the box. Example: 2:00.

①

②

③

④

⑤

⑥

⑦

⑧

⑨

Basic Time Telling – Introducing Hours and Half Hours

Date: _____ Start: _____ Finish: _____ Score: _____

What time does the clock show? Write in the box. Example: 2:00.

①

②

③

④

⑤

⑥

⑦

⑧

⑨

Date: _____ Start: _____ Finish: _____ Score: _____

What time does the clock show? Write in the box. Example: 2:00.

(1)

(2)

(3)

(4)

(5)

(6)

(7)

(8)

(9)

Basic Time Telling – Introducing Hours and Half Hours

Date: _____   Start: _____   Finish: _____   Score: _____

What time does the clock show? Write in the box. Example: 2:00.

1

2

3

4

5

6

7

8

9

Date: _____ Start: _____ Finish: _____ Score: _____

What time does the clock show? Write in the box. Example: 2:00.

(1)

(2)

(3)

(4)

(5)

(6)

(7)

(8)

(9)

Date: _____   Start: _____   Finish: _____   Score: _____

Draw the hands to show the time.

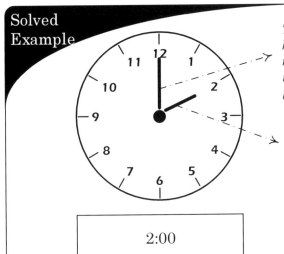

Solved Example

The longer hand that represents the minute should be at 12

The shorter hand that represents the hour should be at 2

Read the time shown in the box. In this case its 2:00. Now using a pencil **draw** hour and minute hands in the clock.

A solved example is shown on the left side.

| 2:00 |

1

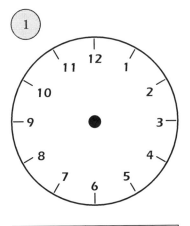

1:00

2

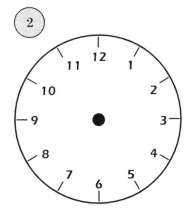

10:00

3

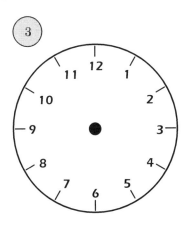

4:00

4

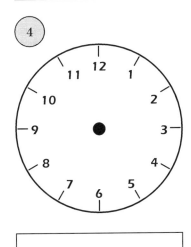

2:00

5

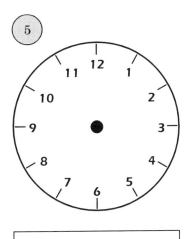

11:00

6

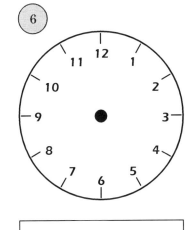

5:00

Date: _____ Start: _____ Finish: _____ Score: _____

Draw the hands to show the time.

1

6:00

2

12:00

3

3:00

4

8:00

5

9:00

6

4:00

7

10:00

8

7:00

9

1:00

Basic Time Telling – Introducing Hours and Half Hours

Date: _____ Start: _____ Finish: _____ Score: _____

Draw the hands to show the time.

(1)

2:00

(2)

12:00

(3)

5:00

(4)

6:00

(5)

11:00

(6)

10:00

(7)

4:00

(8)

3:00

(9)

8:00

Date: _____   Start: _____   Finish: _____   Score: _____

Draw the hands to show the time.

①

8:00

②

3:00

③

11:00

④

6:00

⑤

2:00

⑥

7:00

⑦

5:00

⑧

12:00

⑨

4:00

Date: _____ Start: _____ Finish: _____ Score: _____

Draw the hands to show the time.

1

1:00

2

8:00

3

3:00

4

10:00

5

2:00

6

4:00

7

11:00

8

6:00

9

7:00

Date: _____ Start: _____ Finish: _____ Score: _____

Draw the hands to show the time.

①

12:00

②

1:00

③

3:00

④

10:00

⑤

11:00

⑥

5:00

⑦

7:00

⑧

8:00

⑨

6:00

Basic Time Telling – Introducing Hours and Half Hours

Date: _____ Start: _____ Finish: _____ Score: _____

What time does the clock show? Write in the box.

Solved Example

The longer hand that represents the minute is at 12

The shorter hand that represents the hour is at 5

Read the time shown in the clock and write down the hour in **digits** in the box below.

A solved example is shown on the left side.

$$5:00$$

1

2

3

4

5

6

Basic Time Telling – Introducing Hours and Half Hours   31

Date: _____ Start: _____ Finish: _____ Score: _____

What time does the clock show? Write in the box.

(1)

(2)

(3)

(4)

(5)

(6)

(7)

(8)

(9)

Basic Time Telling – Introducing Hours and Half Hours

Date: _____   Start: _____   Finish: _____   Score: _____

What time does the clock show? Write in the box.

①

②

③

④

⑤

⑥

⑦

⑧

⑨

Date: _____ Start: _____ Finish: _____ Score: _____

What time does the clock show? Write in the box.

1

2

3

4

5

6

7

8

9

Basic Time Telling – Introducing Hours and Half Hours

Date: _____ Start: _____ Finish: _____ Score: _____

Draw the hands to show the time.

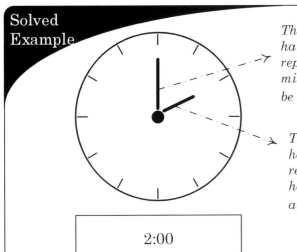

Solved Example

The longer hand that represents the minute should be at 12

The shorter hand that represents the hour should be at 2

2:00

Read the time shown in the box. In this case its 2:00. Now using a pencil **draw** hour and minute hands in the clock.

A solved example is shown on the left side.

①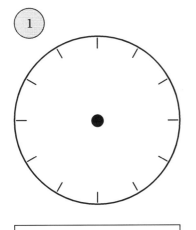

5:00

②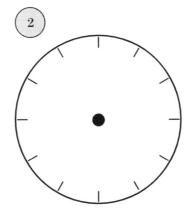

4:00

③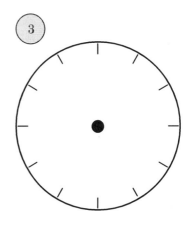

11:00

④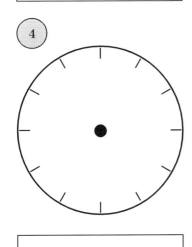

12:00

⑤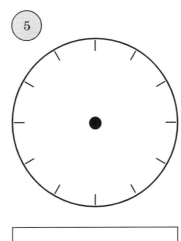

6:00

⑥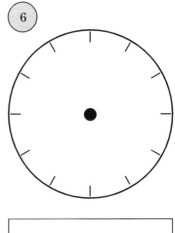

9:00

Date: _____ Start: _____ Finish: _____ Score: _____

Draw the hands to show the time.

1

5:00

2

1:00

3

10:00

4

6:00

5

11:00

6

4:00

7

2:00

8

12:00

9

3:00

Basic Time Telling – Introducing Hours and Half Hours

Date: _____ Start: _____ Finish: _____ Score: _____

Draw the hands to show the time.

1

6:00

2

3:00

3

7:00

4

5:00

5

11:00

6

10:00

7

1:00

8

8:00

9

12:00

Date: _____ Start: _____ Finish: _____ Score: _____

Draw the hands to show the time.

①

7:00

②

6:00

③

10:00

④

5:00

⑤

12:00

⑥

8:00

⑦

4:00

⑧

9:00

⑨

2:00

Basic Time Telling – Introducing Hours and Half Hours

Date: _____ Start: _____ Finish: _____ Score: _____

Match the analog and digital clocks that show the same time.

Solved Example

Read the time shown in the clock on the left and then try to find that time in the box on the right. Once you see a match, draw a line to connect them.

A solved example is shown below.

1

a   `4:00`

2

b   `7:00`

3

c   `3:00`

4

d   `8:00`

5

e   `12:00`

Date: _____ Start: _____ Finish: _____ Score: _____

Match the analog and digital clocks that show the same time.

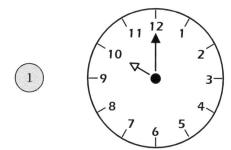

(1)

(A)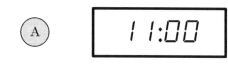

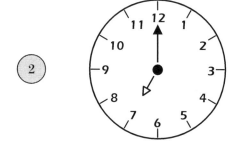

(2)

(B)

(3)

(C)

(4)

(D)

(5)

(E)

Date: _____   Start: _____   Finish: _____   Score: _____

Match the analog and digital clocks that show the same time.

(1)   (A)   08:00

(2)   (B)   03:00

(3)   (C)   10:00

(4)   (D)   06:00

(5)   (E)   01:00

Date: _____ Start: _____ Finish: _____ Score: _____

Match the analog and digital clocks that show the same time.

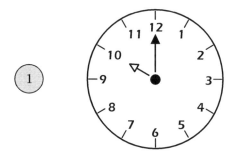

(1)   (A)   05:00

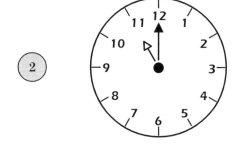

(2)   (B)   10:00

(3)   (C)   07:00

(4)   (D)   11:00

(5)   (E)   02:00

Date: _____   Start: _____   Finish: _____   Score: _____

Match the analog and digital clocks that show the same time.

①    Ⓐ

②    Ⓑ

③    Ⓒ

④   Ⓓ **01:00**

⑤   Ⓔ **03:00**

Date: _____   Start: _____   Finish: _____   Score: _____

Match the analog and digital clocks that show the same time.

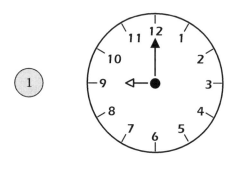

(1)

(A) `02:00`

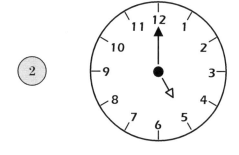

(2)

(B) `05:00`

(3)

(C) `07:00`

(4)

(D) `09:00`

(5)

(E) `10:00`

Date: _____ Start: _____ Finish: _____ Score: _____

Write the time elapsed between two clocks.

Solved Example

Read the start time shown in the clock on the left and then traverse it on the end clock shown in the right to get end time. In below example, you need to traverse 3 hours to get to 7:00 (end time) from 4:00 (start time)

Start Time

End Time

Elapsed Time

3 : 00

1 Start Time

End Time

Elapsed Time

:

2 Start Time

End Time

Elapsed Time

:

3 Start Time

End Time

Elapsed Time

:

Date: _____   Start: _____   Finish: _____   Score: _____

Write the time elapsed between two clocks.

(1)   Start Time   End Time

Elapsed Time

[:]

(2)   Start Time   End Time

Elapsed Time

[:]

(3)   Start Time   End Time

Elapsed Time

[:]

(4)   Start Time   End Time

Elapsed Time

[:]

Date: _____   Start: _____   Finish: _____   Score: _____

Write the time elapsed between two clocks.

1   Start Time   End Time

Elapsed Time

:

2   Start Time   End Time

Elapsed Time

:

3   Start Time   End Time

Elapsed Time

:

4   Start Time   End Time

Elapsed Time

:

Date: _____ Start: _____ Finish: _____ Score: _____

Write the time elapsed between two clocks.

①   Start Time   End Time

Elapsed Time

:

②   Start Time   End Time

Elapsed Time

:

③   Start Time   End Time

Elapsed Time

:

④   Start Time   End Time

Elapsed Time

:

Date: _____ Start: _____ Finish: _____ Score: _____

Write the time elapsed between two clocks.

(1) Start Time   End Time

Elapsed Time

[:]

(2) Start Time   End Time

Elapsed Time

[:]

(3) Start Time   End Time

Elapsed Time

[:]

(4) Start Time   End Time

Elapsed Time

[:]

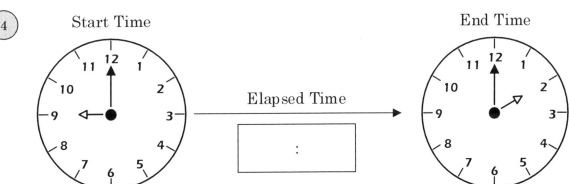

Basic Time Telling – Introducing Hours and Half Hours

Date: _____ Start: _____ Finish: _____ Score: _____

Write the time elapsed between two clocks.

1 Start Time

Elapsed Time

[:]

End Time

2 Start Time

Elapsed Time

[:]

End Time

3 Start Time

Elapsed Time

[:]

End Time

4 Start Time

Elapsed Time

[:]

End Time

Date: _____ Start: _____ Finish: _____ Score: _____

Draw the hands to show the end time.

Solved Example

Read the start time shown in the clock on the left and then traverse it on the end clock shown in the right to get end time. In below example, you need to traverse 3 hours to get to 7:00 (end time) from 4:00 (start time)

Start Time

End Time

Elapsed Time

3:00

1   Start Time

End Time

Elapsed Time

4:00

2   Start Time

End Time

Elapsed Time

1:00

3   Start Time

End Time

Elapsed Time

4:00

Date: _____ Start: _____ Finish: _____ Score: _____

Draw the hands to show the end time.

1 Start Time   End Time

Elapsed Time

4:00

2 Start Time   End Time

Elapsed Time

6:00

3 Start Time   End Time

Elapsed Time

1:00

4 Start Time   End Time

Elapsed Time

6:00

Date: _____ Start: _____ Finish: _____ Score: _____

Draw the hands to show the end time.

(1) Start Time   End Time

Elapsed Time

3:00

(2) Start Time   End Time

Elapsed Time

3:00

(3) Start Time   End Time

Elapsed Time

5:00

(4) Start Time   End Time

Elapsed Time

6:00

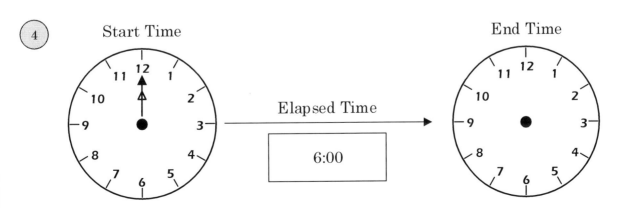

Date: _____   Start: _____   Finish: _____   Score: _____

Draw the hands to show the end time.

(1)   Start Time   End Time

Elapsed Time

1:00

(2)   Start Time   End Time

Elapsed Time

5:00

(3)   Start Time   End Time

Elapsed Time

3:00

(4)   Start Time   End Time

Elapsed Time

5:00

Date: _____ Start: _____ Finish: _____ Score: _____

Draw the hands to show the start time.

Solved Example

Read the end time shown in the clock on the right and then traverse it backwards on the start clock shown in the left to get start time. In below example, you need to traverse 3 hours to get to 4:00 (start time) from 7:00

Start Time

Elapsed Time

3 : 00

End Time

1

Start Time

Elapsed Time

1:00

End Time

2

Start Time

Elapsed Time

6:00

End Time

3

Start Time

Elapsed Time

4:00

End Time

Date: _____   Start: _____   Finish: _____   Score: _____

Draw the hands to show the start time.

1   Start Time

Elapsed Time

4:00

End Time

2   Start Time

Elapsed Time

2:00

End Time

3   Start Time

Elapsed Time

2:00

End Time

4   Start Time

Elapsed Time

5:00

End Time

Basic Time Telling – Introducing Hours and Half Hours

Date: _____   Start: _____   Finish: _____   Score: _____

Draw the hands to show the start time.

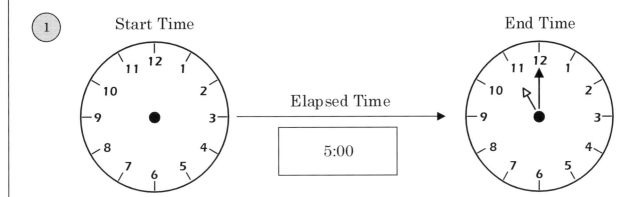

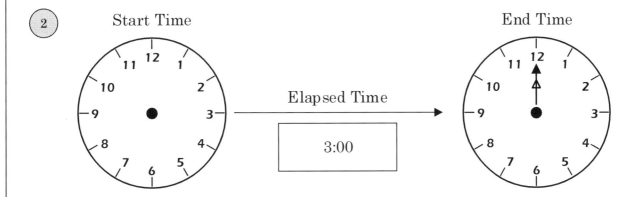

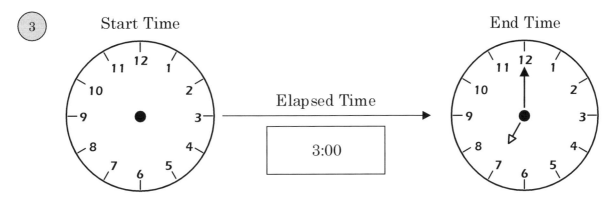

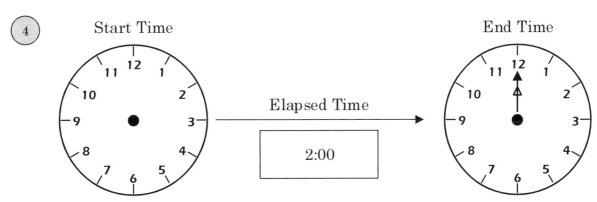

Date: _____ Start: _____ Finish: _____ Score: _____

Draw the hands to show the start time.

1 Start Time

Elapsed Time

5:00

End Time

2 Start Time

Elapsed Time

2:00

End Time

3 Start Time

Elapsed Time

2:00

End Time

4 Start Time

Elapsed Time

6:00

End Time

Basic Time Telling – Introducing Hours and Half Hours

Date: _____   Start: _____   Finish: _____   Score: _____

Circle the clock indicating the correct time.

Solved Example Ashley started playing with her friends at 7:00. She played for 2 hours. Which clock below shows the time she finished playing?

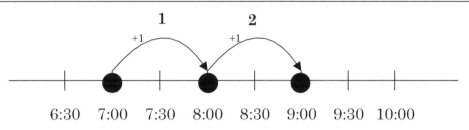

6:30   7:00   7:30   8:00   8:30   9:00   9:30   10:00

Ashley started playing at 7:00 and since she played for 2 hours, we need to add 2 hours to 7:00. So the answer is the third clock from the left that shows 9:00

1 The class was given 2 hours to complete the assignment. What time will the assignment need to be completed if the teacher handed out the assignment at 01:00 PM?

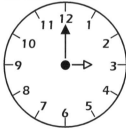 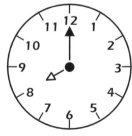  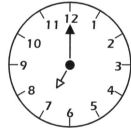

2 Angela decided to take a science class. The class started at 01:00 PM and lasted for 2 hours. What time did the class end?

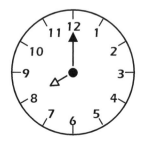 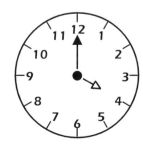 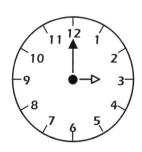 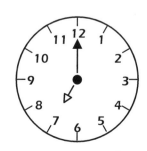

Date: _____   Start: _____   Finish: _____   Score: _____

Circle the clock indicating the correct time.

① Xavier goes for a 2 hours bike ride every day. Today, he begins his ride at 09:00 AM. What time will Xavier finish riding his bike?

② Angelica decided to write a letter to her grandfather. After spending an hour she could finish writing at 07:00 PM. What time was it when Angelica started writing the letter?

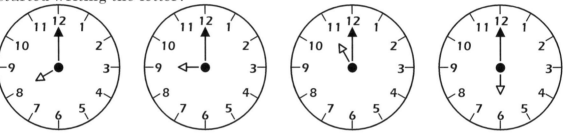

③ Faith was going on a vacation to Florida. Her flight is scheduled to depart at 09:00 AM and is expected to take 3 hours to reach Orlando. What time the plane is scheduled to land?

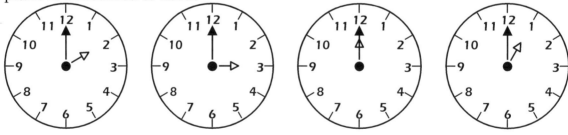

④ Lucy begins her morning walk at 08:00 AM. She walks for an hour. What time is Lucy done walking?

Date: _____   Start: _____   Finish: _____   Score: _____

Circle the clock indicating the correct time.

1. It took Abby an hour to walk to the school. What time did Abby arrive at the school if she started at 09:00 AM?

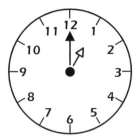 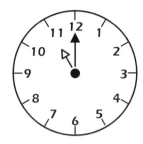 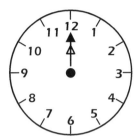 

2. Claire and Julianna just finished watching a movie for 2 hours. If they started watching the movie at 04:00 PM what time the clock shows now?

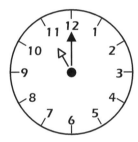 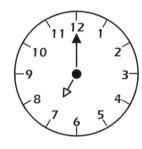 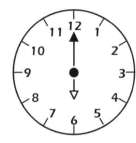 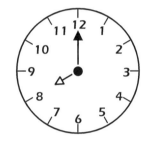

3. It takes 2 hours for Hope's dad to repair a broken truck. He finished repairing at 02:00 PM. What time he started?

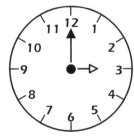 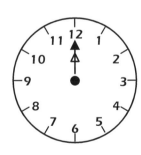  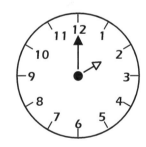

4. The class was given 2 hours to complete the assignment. What time will the assignment need to be completed if the teacher handed out the assignment at 12:00 PM?

 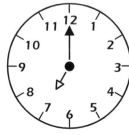  

Date: _____   Start: _____   Finish: _____   Score: _____

Circle the clock indicating the correct time.

1 Gabriela watched a 3 hours TV show yesterday. What time did the TV show begin if Gabriela finished watching it at 10:00 PM?

2 Nicolas arrived at a restaurant for dinner at 07:00 PM. He placed his order, ate, and paid the bill. He left the restaurant 2 hours later. What time was it when Nicolas left the restaurant?

3 Ellie watched a fireworks show. The first firework went off at 07:00 PM. She watched until the show ended 2 hours later. What time was it when the fireworks show ended?

  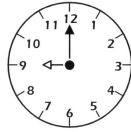 

4 Michelle decided to take a science class. The class started at 12:00 PM and lasted for 2 hours. What time did the class end?

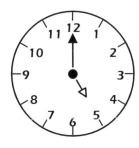 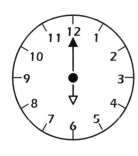 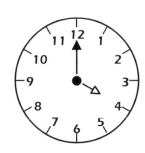

Basic Time Telling – Introducing Hours and Half Hours

Date:_____   Start:_____   Finish:_____   Score:_____

Circle the clock indicating the correct time.

1 Bailey left school at 03:00 PM. It takes her an hour to reach home. When will she get home?

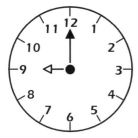 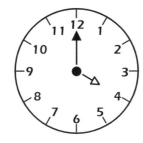 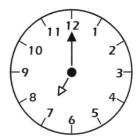 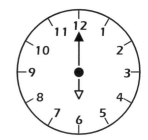

2 The class was given 2 hours to complete the assignment. What time will the assignment need to be completed if the teacher handed out the assignment at 12:00 PM?

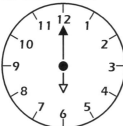   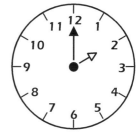

3 Oscar was preparing for a report presentation at his school. His old printer takes an hour to print a report. If he was done printing at 04:00 PM, what time did he start printing the report?

 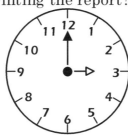  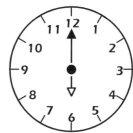

4 Raymond arrived at a restaurant for dinner at 07:00 PM. He placed his order, ate, and paid the bill. He left the restaurant 2 hours later. What time was it when Raymond left the restaurant?

Date: _____   Start: _____   Finish: _____   Score: _____

Circle the clock indicating the correct time.

① Wyatt goes for a an hour bike ride every day. Today, he begins his ride at 09:00 AM. What time will Wyatt finish riding his bike?

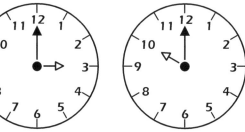

② Maggie begins her morning walk at 09:00 AM. She walks for 2 hours. What time is Maggie done walking?

③ Gerardo was preparing for a report presentation at his school. His old printer takes an hour to print a report. If he was done printing at 04:00 PM, what time did he start printing the report?

④ Giselle started for library along with her brother Kevin at 11:00 AM. It took her 2 hours in the line to return books. What time did they return the books?

Date: _____ Start: _____ Finish: _____ Score: _____

Draw the missing hands as per the time pattern.

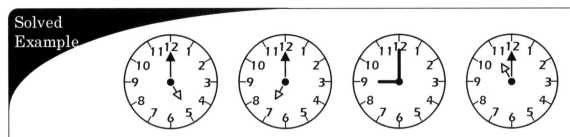

Solved
Example

The time elapsed between first and second clock is 2 hours and if we add the same elapsed time of 2 hours to second clock, the third clock reads 9:00. Now the third and fourth clock also have 2 hours of elapsed time between them.

So the third clock should show 9:00. Draw as shown above in the third clock from the left.

Date: _____ Start: _____ Finish: _____ Score: _____

Draw the missing hands as per the time pattern.

Basic Time Telling – Introducing Hours and Half Hours

Date: _____   Start: _____   Finish: _____   Score: _____

Draw the missing hands as per the time pattern.

Date: _____   Start: _____   Finish: _____   Score: _____

Draw the missing hands as per the time pattern.

Date: _____ Start: _____ Finish: _____ Score: _____

What time does the clock show? Fill the box. Example: Half past two.

1

2

3

4

5

6

7

8

9

Basic Time Telling – Introducing Hours and Half Hours

Date: _____ Start: _____ Finish: _____ Score: _____

What time does the clock show? Fill the box. Example: Half past two.

①

②

③

④

⑤

⑥

⑦

⑧

⑨

Basic Time Telling – Introducing Hours and Half Hours

Date: _____ Start: _____ Finish: _____ Score: _____

What time does the clock show? Fill the box. Example: Half past two.

(1)

[clock 1]

(2)

[clock 2]

(3)

[clock 3]

(4)

[clock 4]

(5)

[clock 5]

(6)

[clock 6]

(7)

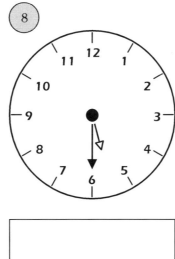

(8)

(9)

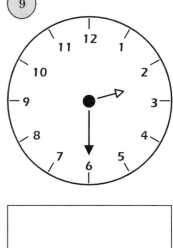

Date: _____ Start: _____ Finish: _____ Score: _____

What time does the clock show? Fill the box. Example: Half past two.

①

②

③

④

⑤

⑥

⑦

⑧

⑨

Date: _____ Start: _____ Finish: _____ Score: _____

Draw the hands to show the time.

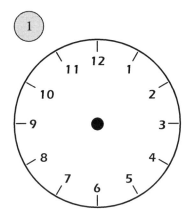

Half past six

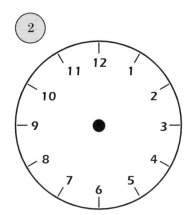

Half past three

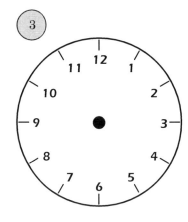

Half past twelve

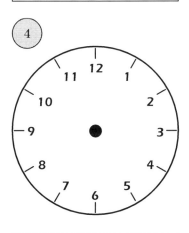

Half past nine

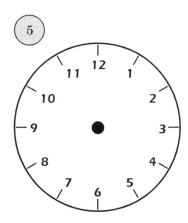

Half past eleven

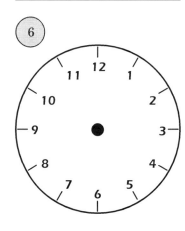

Half past four

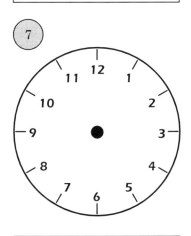

Half past eight

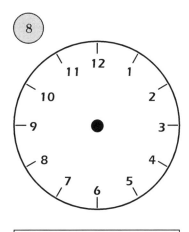

Half past two

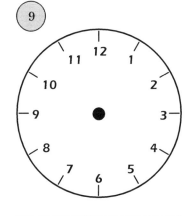

Half past five

Date: _____ Start: _____ Finish: _____ Score: _____

Draw the hands to show the time.

1	2	3
Half past four	Half past ten	Half past eleven

4	5	6
Half past three	Half past seven	Half past twelve

7	8	9
Half past five	Half past eight	Half past six

Date:_____ Start:_____ Finish:_____ Score:_____

What time does the clock show? Write in the box. Example: 2:30.

①

②

③

④

⑤

⑥

⑦

⑧

⑨

Date: _____ Start: _____ Finish: _____ Score: _____

What time does the clock show? Write in the box. Example: 2:30.

1

2

3

4

5

6

7

8

9

Basic Time Telling – Introducing Hours and Half Hours

Date:_____ Start:_____ Finish:_____ Score:_____

What time does the clock show? Write in the box. Example: 2:30.

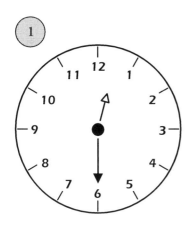

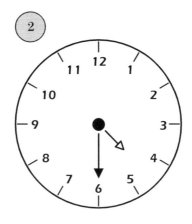

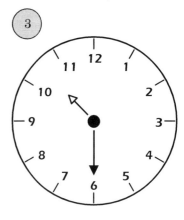

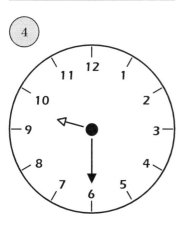

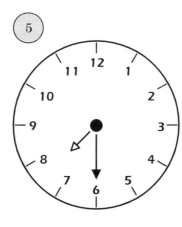

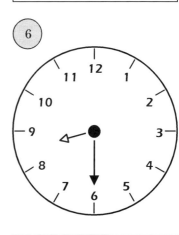

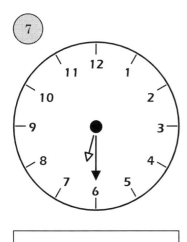

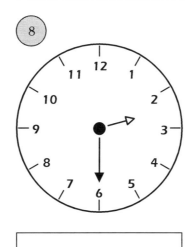

Date:_____ Start:_____ Finish:_____ Score:_____

What time does the clock show? Write in the box. Example: 2:30.

①

②

③

④

⑤

⑥

⑦

⑧

⑨

Date: _____ Start: _____ Finish: _____ Score: _____

Draw the hands to show the time.

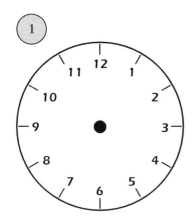

6:30

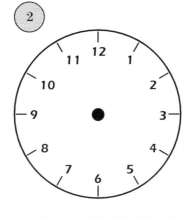

12:30

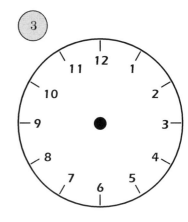

2:30

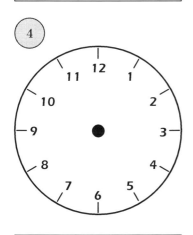

9:30

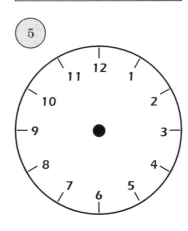

10:30

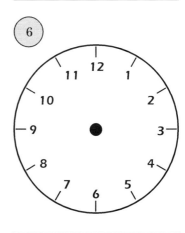

4:30

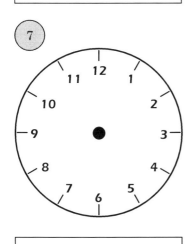

11:30

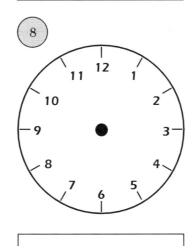

5:30

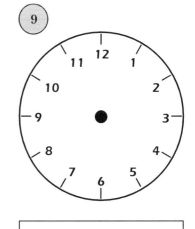

1:30

Date: _____ Start: _____ Finish: _____ Score: _____

Draw the hands to show the time.

①

8:30

②

1:30

③

2:30

④

5:30

⑤

3:30

⑥

10:30

⑦

7:30

⑧

9:30

⑨

11:30

Date: _____   Start: _____   Finish: _____   Score: _____

What time does the clock show? Write in the box.

1

2

3

4

5

6

7

8

9

Date: _____ Start: _____ Finish: _____ Score: _____

What time does the clock show? Write in the box.

1

2

3

4

5

6

7

8

9

Basic Time Telling – Introducing Hours and Half Hours

Date:_____ Start:_____ Finish:_____ Score:_____

Draw the hands to show the time.

①

3:30

②

5:30

③

2:30

④

12:30

⑤

11:30

⑥

9:30

⑦

4:30

⑧

10:30

⑨

1:30

Basic Time Telling – Introducing Hours and Half Hours

Date: _____ Start: _____ Finish: _____ Score: _____

Draw the hands to show the time.

①

5:30

②

3:30

③

1:30

④

11:30

⑤

7:30

⑥

6:30

⑦

12:30

⑧

9:30

⑨

4:30

Basic Time Telling – Introducing Hours and Half Hours

Date: _____ Start: _____ Finish: _____ Score: _____

Match the analog and digital clocks that show the same time.

(1)

(A)  `06:30`

(2)

(B)  `05:30`

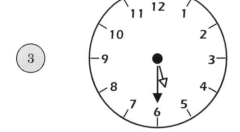

(3)

(C)  `02:30`

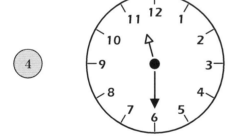

(4)

(D)  `11:30`

(5)

(E) `01:30`

Date: _____ Start: _____ Finish: _____ Score: _____

Match the analog and digital clocks that show the same time.

(1)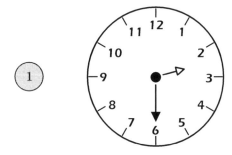

(A)

(2)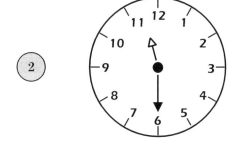

(B)

(3)

(C)

(4)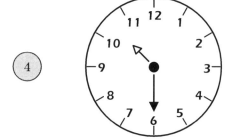

(D) 04:30

(5)

(E) 11:30

Basic Time Telling – Introducing Hours and Half Hours

Date: _____ Start: _____ Finish: _____ Score: _____

Write the time elapsed between two clocks.

1 Start Time   End Time

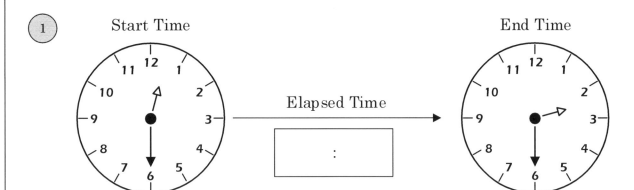

Elapsed Time

2 Start Time   End Time

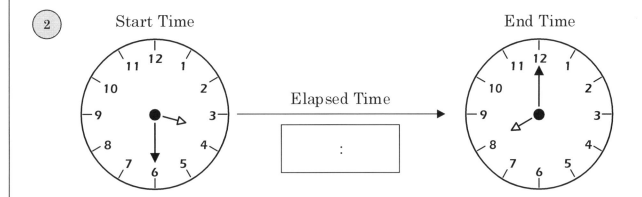

Elapsed Time

3 Start Time   End Time

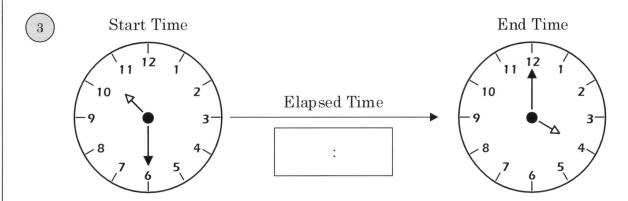

Elapsed Time

4 Start Time   End Time

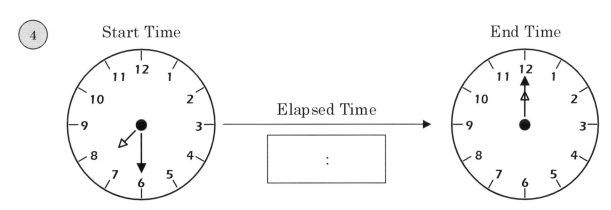

Elapsed Time

Date: _____ Start: _____ Finish: _____ Score: _____

Write the time elapsed between two clocks.

1 Start Time   End Time

Elapsed Time

[:]

2 Start Time   End Time

Elapsed Time

[:]

3 Start Time   End Time

Elapsed Time

[:]

4 Start Time   End Time

Elapsed Time

[:]

Date: _____ Start: _____ Finish: _____ Score: _____

Write the time elapsed between two clocks.

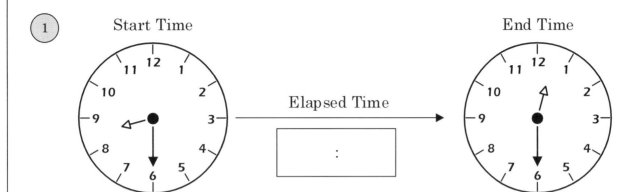

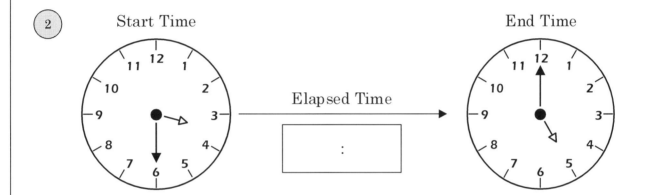

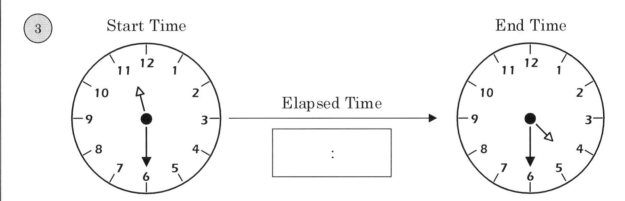

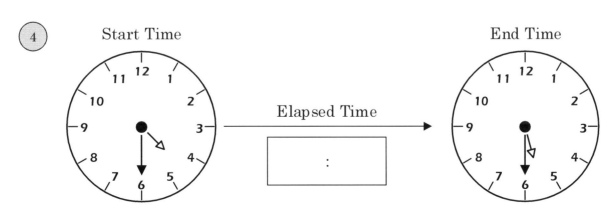

Date: _____   Start: _____   Finish: _____   Score: _____

Write the time elapsed between two clocks.

(1)   Start Time   End Time

Elapsed Time

[:]

(2)   Start Time   End Time

Elapsed Time

[:]

(3)   Start Time   End Time

Elapsed Time

[:]

(4)   Start Time   End Time

Elapsed Time

[:]

Basic Time Telling – Introducing Hours and Half Hours

Date: _____ Start: _____ Finish: _____ Score: _____

Draw the hands to show the end time.

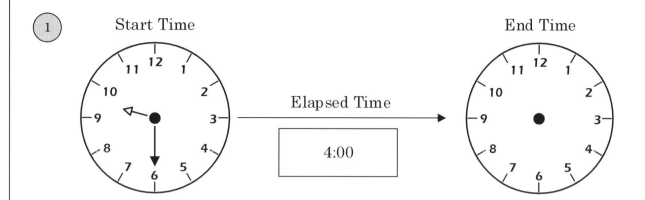

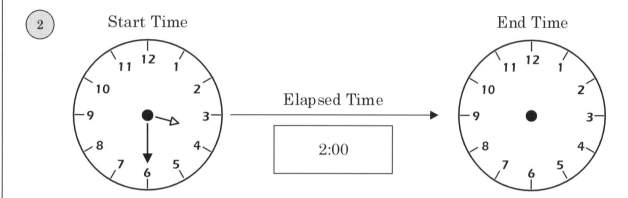

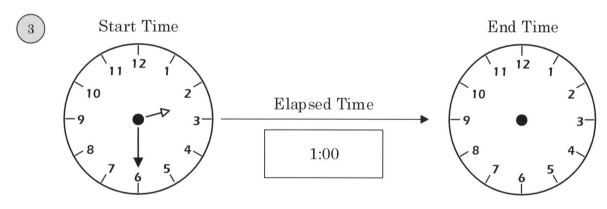

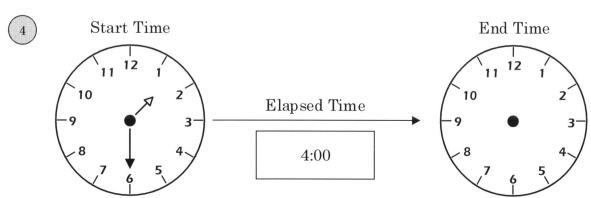

Date: _____ Start: _____ Finish: _____ Score: _____

Draw the hands to show the end time.

(1) Start Time   End Time

Elapsed Time

4:00

(2) Start Time   End Time

Elapsed Time

2:00

(3) Start Time   End Time

Elapsed Time

4:00

(4) Start Time   End Time

Elapsed Time

4:00

Date:_____ Start:_____ Finish:_____ Score:_____

Draw the hands to show the start time.

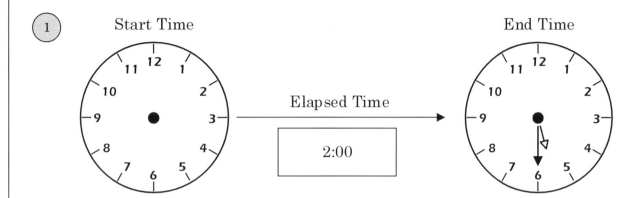

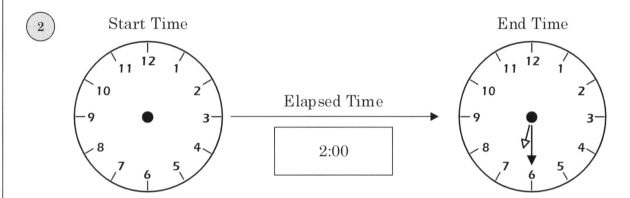

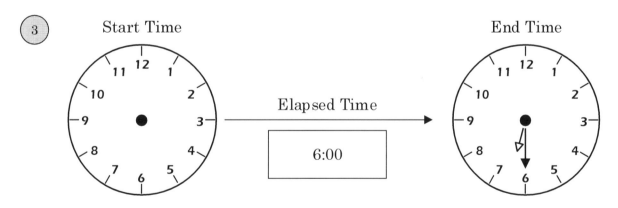

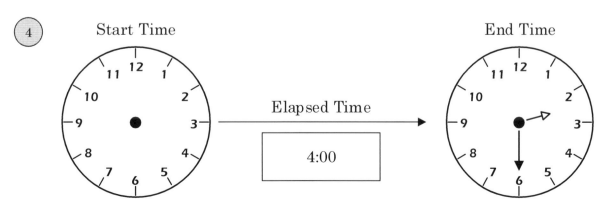

Date: _____ Start: _____ Finish: _____ Score: _____

Draw the hands to show the start time.

(1) Start Time   End Time

Elapsed Time

5:00

(2) Start Time   End Time

Elapsed Time

4:00

(3) Start Time   End Time

Elapsed Time

2:00

(4) Start Time   End Time

Elapsed Time

2:00

Date:_____   Start:_____   Finish:_____   Score:_____

Circle the clock indicating the correct time.

1. Dakota left school at 02:30 PM. It takes her 30 minutes to reach home. When will she get home?

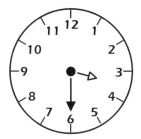 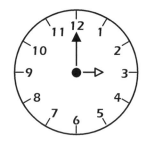 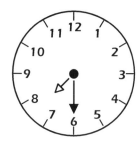 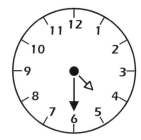

2. Monica works for 6 hours and 30 minutes a day at a local library. If she begins work at 08:30 AM, what time will Monica go home?

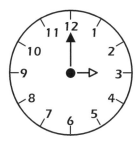 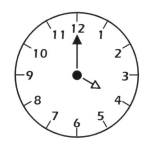  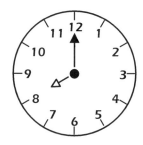

3. Fernando goes for a an hour and 30 minutes bike ride every day. Today, he begins his ride at 07:30 AM. What time will Fernando finish riding his bike?

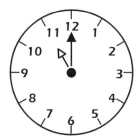  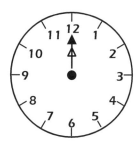 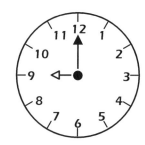

4. Mckenzie decided to write a letter to her grandfather. After spending an hour she could finish writing at 07:00 PM. What time was it when Mckenzie started writing the letter?

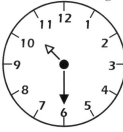 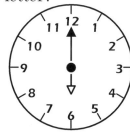 

Date:_____   Start:_____   Finish:_____   Score:_____

Circle the clock indicating the correct time.

(1) Jordan begins her morning walk at 06:30 AM. She walks for an hour. What time is Jordan done walking?

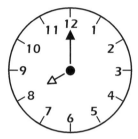 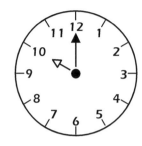 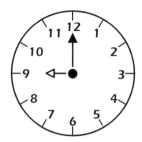 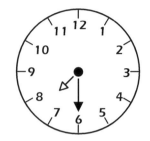

(2) Arianna watched her favorite TV show for 30 minutes, if she finished watching the show at 05:30 PM, what time did she start watching?

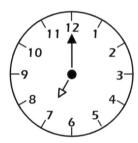 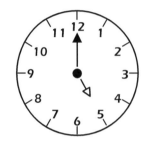 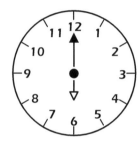 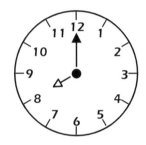

(3) Bianca watched a 2 hours TV show yesterday. What time did the TV show begin if Bianca finished watching it at 09:00 PM?

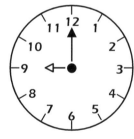  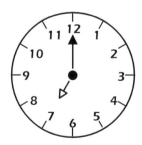 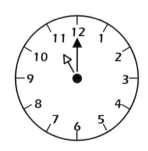

(4) Jacqueline decided to write a letter to her grandfather. After spending an hour she could finish writing at 07:00 PM. What time was it when Jacqueline started writing the letter?

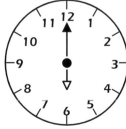  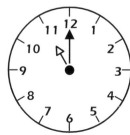

Date: _____ Start: _____ Finish: _____ Score: _____

Draw the missing hands as per the time pattern.

Date: _____ Start: _____ Finish: _____ Score: _____

Draw the missing hands as per the time pattern.

Basic Time Telling – Introducing Hours and Half Hours

Answer Key

Page 7

1. Twelve O'Clock
2. Three O'Clock
3. Eleven O'Clock
4. Two O'Clock
5. One O'Clock
6. Eight O'Clock

Page 8

1. Twelve O'Clock
2. Three O'Clock
3. Five O'Clock
4. Six O'Clock
5. Nine O'Clock
6. Eleven O'Clock
7. Seven O'Clock
8. One O'Clock
9. Eight O'Clock

Page 9

1. Ten O'Clock
2. Two O'Clock
3. Five O'Clock
4. Three O'Clock
5. Nine O'Clock
6. Eleven O'Clock
7. Seven O'Clock
8. Twelve O'Clock
9. One O'Clock

Page 10

1. Four O'Clock
2. Nine O'Clock
3. Six O'Clock
4. One O'Clock
5. Twelve O'Clock
6. Three O'Clock

7. Eight O'Clock
8. Five O'Clock
9. Two O'Clock

Page 11

1. Seven O'Clock
2. Four O'Clock
3. Five O'Clock
4. Three O'Clock
5. One O'Clock
6. Two O'Clock
7. Nine O'Clock
8. Eleven O'Clock
9. Eight O'Clock

Page 12

1. Seven O'Clock
2. Two O'Clock
3. Eight O'Clock
4. Nine O'Clock
5. Six O'Clock
6. Eleven O'Clock
7. Three O'Clock
8. Four O'Clock
9. Five O'Clock

Page 13

1.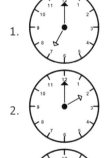

2.

3.

4.

5.

6.

Page 14

1.

2.

3.

4.

5.

6.

7.

8.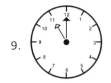

9.

Page 15

1.

2.

3.

4.

5.

6.

7.

8.

9.

Page 16

1.

2.

3.

4.

5.

6.

7.

8.

9.

Page 17

1.

2.

3.

4.

5.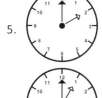

6.

7.

8.

9.

Page 18

1.

2.

3.

4.

5.

6.

7.

8.

9.

Page 19

1. 7:00
2. 2:00
3. 4:00
4. 11:00
5. 5:00
6. 6:00

Page 20

1. 9:00
2. 10:00
3. 5:00
4. 3:00
5. 1:00
6. 8:00
7. 6:00
8. 7:00

9. 12:00

Page 21

1. 11:00
2. 1:00
3. 12:00
4. 5:00
5. 4:00
6. 3:00
7. 6:00
8. 2:00
9. 10:00

Page 22

1. 7:00
2. 12:00
3. 10:00
4. 3:00
5. 6:00
6. 8:00
7. 1:00
8. 4:00
9. 9:00

Page 23

1. 2:00
2. 12:00
3. 3:00
4. 10:00
5. 7:00
6. 11:00
7. 5:00
8. 4:00
9. 9:00

Page 24

1. 1:00
2. 10:00

3. 12:00
4. 7:00
5. 2:00
6. 6:00
7. 4:00
8. 8:00
9. 3:00

Page 25

1.

2.

3.

4.

5.

6.

Page 26

1.

2.

3.

4.

5.

6.

7.

8.

9.

Page 27

1.

2.

3.

4.

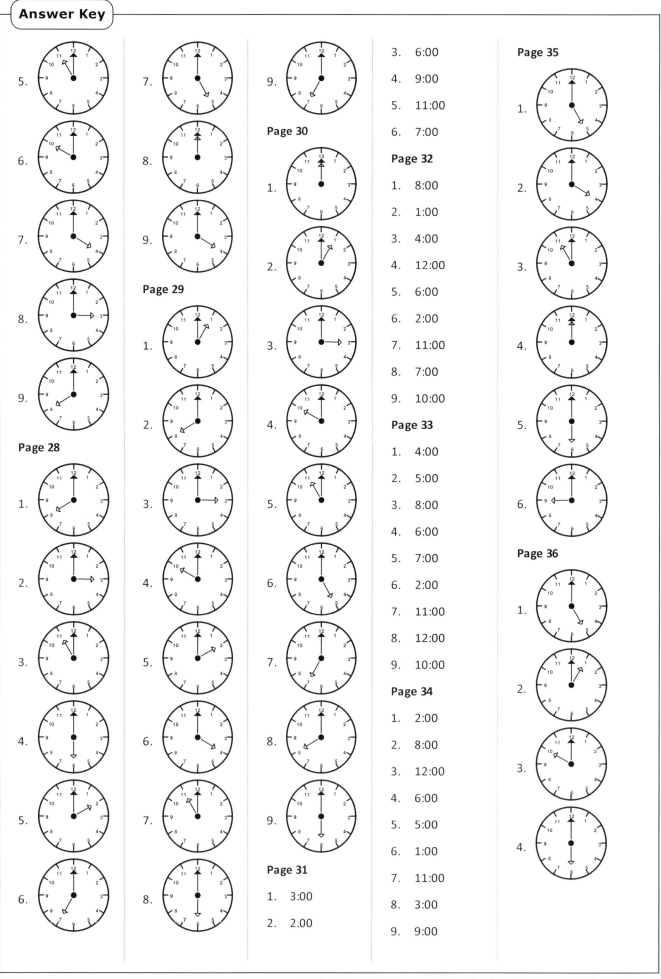

5.

6.

7.

8.

9.

Page 28

1.

2.

3.

4.

5.

6.

7.

8.

9.

Page 29

1.

2.

3.

4.

5.

6.

7.

8.

9.

Page 30

1.

2.

3.

4.

5.

6.

7.

8.

9.

Page 31

1. 3:00

2. 2:00

3. 6:00

4. 9:00

5. 11:00

6. 7:00

Page 32

1. 8:00

2. 1:00

3. 4:00

4. 12:00

5. 6:00

6. 2:00

7. 11:00

8. 7:00

9. 10:00

Page 33

1. 4:00

2. 5:00

3. 8:00

4. 6:00

5. 7:00

6. 2:00

7. 11:00

8. 12:00

9. 10:00

Page 34

1. 2:00

2. 8:00

3. 12:00

4. 6:00

5. 5:00

6. 1:00

7. 11:00

8. 3:00

9. 9:00

Page 35

1.

2.

3.

4.

5.

6.

Page 36

1.

2.

3.

4.

5.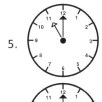

6.

7.

8.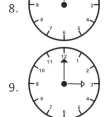

9.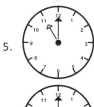

Page 37

1.

2.

3.

4.

5.

6.

7.

8.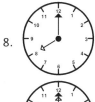

9.

Page 38

1.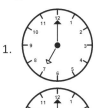

2.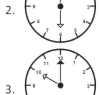

3.

4.

5.

6.

7.

8.

9.

Page 40

1. 1 --> B
2. 2 --> C
3. 3 --> A
4. 4 --> E
5. 5 --> D

Page 41

1. 1 --> B
2. 2 --> D
3. 3 --> C
4. 4 --> E
5. 5 --> A

Page 42

1. 1 --> B
2. 2 --> D
3. 3 --> C
4. 4 --> A
5. 5 --> E

Page 43

1. 1 --> C
2. 2 --> D
3. 3 --> A
4. 4 --> E
5. 5 --> B

Page 44

1. 1 --> D
2. 2 --> B
3. 3 --> E
4. 4 --> C
5. 5 --> A

Page 45

1. 2:00
2. 2:00
3. 3:00

Page 46

1. 2:00
2. 2:00
3. 5:00
4. 3:00

Page 47

1. 3:00
2. 5:00
3. 5:00
4. 3:00

Page 48

1. 2:00
2. 2:00
3. 5:00
4. 5:00

Page 49

1. 2:00
2. 3:00
3. 3:00
4. 5:00

Page 50

1. 6:00
2. 2:00
3. 3:00
4. 5:00

Page 51

1.

2.

3.

Page 52

1.

2.

3.

4.

Page 53

1.

2.

3.

4.

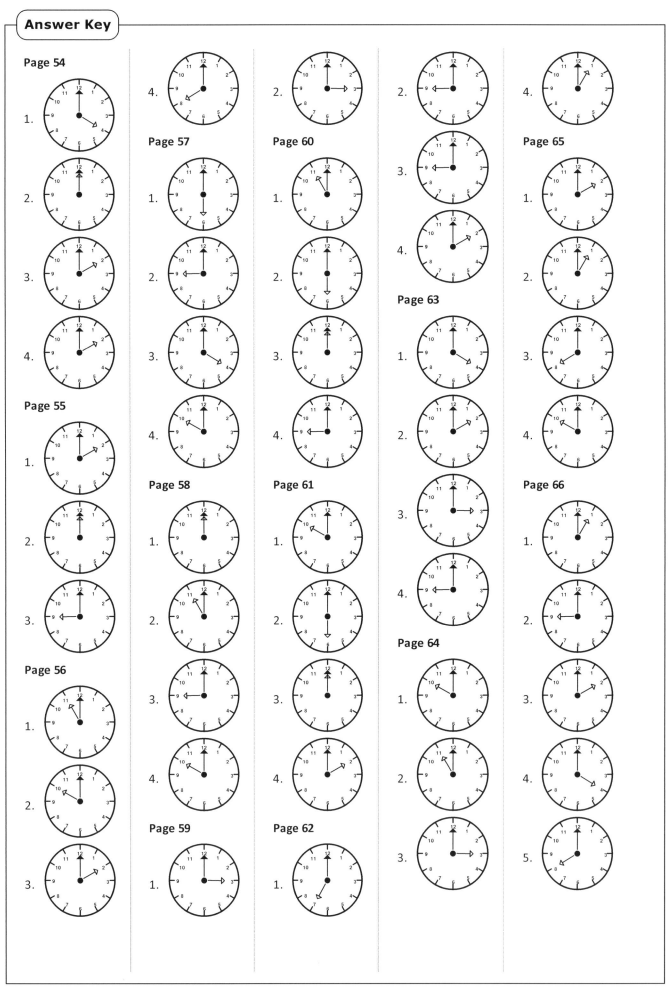

Page 54

Page 55

Page 56

Page 57

Page 58

Page 59

Page 60

Page 61

Page 62

Page 63

Page 64

Page 65

Page 66

Basic Time Telling – Introducing Hours and Half Hours

6.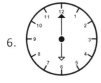

Page 67

1.

2.

3.

4.

5.

6.

Page 68

1.

2.

3.

4.

5.

6.

Page 69

1. Half past eight

2. Half past three

3. Half past seven

4. Half past four

5. Half past twelve

6. Half past one

7. Half past ten

8. Half past eleven

9. Half past five

Page 70

1. Half past four

2. Half past two

3. Half past seven

4. Half past eight

5. Half past six

6. Half past twelve

7. Half past five

8. Half past eleven

9. Half past nine

Page 71

1. Half past nine

2. Half past ten

3. Half past twelve

4. Half past eight

5. Half past three

6. Half past one

7. Half past six

8. Half past five

9. Half past two

Page 72

1. Half past one

2. Half past two

3. Half past twelve

4. Half past ten

5. Half past four

6. Half past eight

7. Half past nine

8. Half past eleven

9. Half past five

Page 73

1.

2.

3.

4.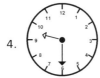

5.

6.

7.

8.

9.

Page 74

1.

2.

3.

4.

5.

6.

7.

8.

Basic Time Telling – Introducing Hours and Half Hours

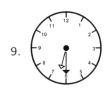

9.

Page 75

1. 8:30
2. 6:30
3. 2:30
4. 7:30
5. 5:30
6. 4:30
7. 3:30
8. 12:30
9. 1:30

Page 76

1. 1:30
2. 3:30
3. 5:30
4. 7:30
5. 6:30
6. 4:30
7. 9:30
8. 10:30
9. 2:30

Page 77

1. 12:30
2. 4:30
3. 10:30
4. 9:30
5. 7:30
6. 8:30
7. 6:30
8. 2:30
9. 1:30

Page 78

1. 8:30
2. 4:30
3. 2:30
4. 6:30
5. 1:30
6. 12:30
7. 7:30
8. 9:30
9. 3:30

Page 79

1.
2.
3.
4.
5.
6.
7.

8.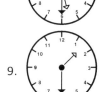

9.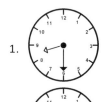

Page 80

1.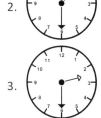
2.
3.
4.
5.
6.
7.
8.
9.

Page 81

1. 12:30
2. 7:30
3. 4:30
4. 3:30
5. 6:30
6. 11:30
7. 8:30
8. 5:30
9. 1:30

Page 82

1. 1:30
2. 7:30
3. 6:30
4. 2:30
5. 4:30
6. 12:30
7. 3:30
8. 10:30
9. 8:30

Page 83

1.
2.
3.
4.

5.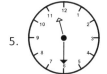

6.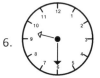

7.

8.

9.

Page 84

1.
2.
3.
4.
5.
6.

7.

8.

9.

Page 85

1. 1 --> A
2. 2 --> E
3. 3 --> B
4. 4 --> D
5. 5 --> C

Page 86

1. 1 --> A
2. 2 --> E
3. 3 --> D
4. 4 --> C
5. 5 --> B

Page 87

1. 2:00
2. 4:30
3. 5:30
4. 4:30

Page 88

1. 1:30
2. 3:30
3. 1:30
4. 1:30

Page 89

1. 4:00
2. 1:30

3. 5:00
4. 1:00

Page 90

1. 1:00
2. 4:00
3. 4:30
4. 1:30

Page 91

1.

2.

3.

4.

Page 92

1.

2.

3.

4.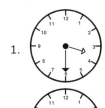

Page 93

1.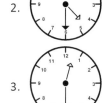

2.

3.

4.

Page 94

1.

2.

3.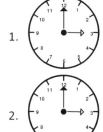

4.

Page 95

1.

2.

3.

4.

Page 96

1.

2.

3.

4.

Page 97

1.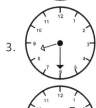

2.

3.

4.

Page 98

1.

2.

3.

4.

5.

6.

Made in the USA
Middletown, DE
11 March 2017